IN-DIFFERENT TIMES OF CHAOS!

TRUE CRIME STORIES

JUSTIN BROUGHTON

A catalogue record for this
work is available from the
National Library of Australia

Broughton, Justin (author)
IN-DIFFERENT TIMES OF CHAOS!
ISBN 978-1-922527-56-1
SHORT STORIES
Typeset Acumin Pro Thin 12/18
Cover and book design by Green Hill Publishing
Cover illustration by Adobe Stock

**I would like to dedicate this book,
to firstly myself and foremost!**
To the love and support from Ronald,
Lorraine and Belinda and
to all those people who always said,
I'd amount to nothing!
Thank them all the most!!!!
But mainly, like I said in the
beginning and end, thanks to all
of mine for helping get me here!!!

FIRE SCAPE

t's finally reached the weekend and I had been at work by myself for most of the week. I worked as an apprentice spray painter/panel beater in the earth moving equipment industry. Anyway, I had been trying to reach my uncle all week long and had heard no response back. I was getting rather concerned something terrible might have happened, he lived a good hours drive from where we worked. I had finally finished spraying and put back together the new machine, which needed touching up from all the parts of assembly. It was getting closer to the machine's pick up deadline and delivery from sale to site, yet with every spray of paint from my spray can all I could keep thinking was I do hope my family's alright.

So with every twist and turn from me unbolting then bolting the nuts and bolts up so they were now tight, I couldn't stop wondering where, how and why my uncle was out of sight. My heart fiercely picked up the pace, it was now in a race with my bolts and all were getting tightened correctly.

I was overthinking, my uncle
needed help, I must move more
like "white lightning". Spanners all
moved, can I fit this damn mirror
then I moved onto the bonnet
thinking once again if I move
quicker than the nut I'm to screw
like a real bee flew out my bum.
Move quicker, then the thought
of my uncle needing me more
than a bee just flew and helped
me put all of these parts back to
the machine all fresh painted and
new. I knew someone needs you I
heard or I thought sweat dripping,
I'm flipping out with all I've been
taught! If anything should happen

to you that bee now took off to take
a look see, before now I hear from
hey what unc unc is that you????
No pressure is for you as I feel I'm
nearly done with this machine as I
worked quicker than a cough syrup
on I flew, blew up more paint pulled
off all the masking tape! Machine
is now ready, take fellas I yelled
I'm in a hurry as I feel something's
wrong. I must get outta here, I
clean sweep all the spray booth
and thought I'm not far from you
unc, just zipping through cleaning
up all this junk, in the bin you go
if anyone has sinned toward my
family I threw more rubbish went

in my was filled with more than the
clean swept spray booth. Splished
and splashed put fine tooth nailed
those spray guns are clean from all,
ohhhhh ohhhhhh my uncle may
need air!!! Who said it, I screamed
I've gone more nuttier than these
spray guns I just cleaned. Bang,
bang cupboards are shut I'm in
a rage nearly done I blew up, is
anything wrong 'I just, IIII jusssssst
can't get through!!!!!! Where the
hell must you be? I'm finally done
to throw on the padlock to lock
all of these, I'm finally free jump
on the blower hey unc are you
tttthhhhhhhheeeeeerrrrrrrrrreeeeeee!!!!

Head full of steam I can chug a
jug we never missed a Friday after
beer!!!! What the hell it was wrong,
I think I just pulled out in front of fifth
gear, how did stear with left smoke
in the rear!!!!!! My family needs me
as I feel the crunching of my now
4 speed gear, thought I had five all
for quicker I thought to arrive. Bang,
bang my heart had jumped clear,
think I left a brown stain in the rear.
Ohh nooooo ohhhhhh I need fuel
as I dual the hot road thinking, hey,
hey you where's my uncle I shout.
I'm on my way no one's else is
quicker!!!!! I made it halfway now
to your house that takes normally

an hour be there in 10 only left 15
ago. Think I ran over a man or a
nan not even the nun I had hit, she
blew flyby eeeeewwwww what's
that there left in the back street?
Don't know as my head Flores
it went into the backseat, have
a fishers friend as I now think of
my uncle not even a beer to pour
down my now missing back seat
throat. I'm finally nearly there, uncle.
I somehow nearly manage to pull
up just shy of his front gate post!!!!
Is he home, I thought as I pulled
out front his home, normally we are
half full our Friday Tooey's stout,
instead I've had a fine stoush with

all that got in my way as I headed
up the hwy. Never before seen,
had I ever been in shock seen the
wind blew or my ford, "FLYBYE all
that well as that poor man back
there even blew off his fake tan and
mouusssssssssstaacccchhhheee
just to get here faster. Now where
ohhhhh yeeehhhhhh where are
you uncle I screamed and shouted,
haven't heard or seen in a few days
now mannnnnnnn, as I ran down
his steep driveway all to find him
ohhhh ohhhhh your there!!!!

He looked flat and tired
as if he had not slept in a week,

'hey uncle,' I said 'you've got a
visitor, yessss it's me your neph
neph neph.' Really all I thought
was the other of nephewww
phew pheeewww worried sick
as I couldn't get through, haven't
even had a sip or suck outt of our
rather routines do a frother! Cheer
up Charlie Justin that tore up the
road and battled all week working
alone, kick back make me a snack
I'll go grab a six and down a few
while you unhinge or unwind
as no contact. I thought I had a
screw loose, put that last machine
I painted for ya quicker than
footloose was a goose. Anyway

how the how the fffff how issssss yaaaaaaaa?

So we briefly get chatting there for a few minutes when his phone rings, so I head down the grog shop whilst he's busy for half an hour, so anyway as I walked up the freshly concreted driveway I was suddenly brought back to life as I now know he's not dead and we can finally have a beer when I get back. So I head down the local when I see this hot hotel worker behind the bottle shop counter and so I swiftly pounced on such a gorgeous look of a

gift of surely sore semen from
her father's loins. I did shout, she
laughed and giggled and put on
a smile.

'Hey so what's the G O
around this joint, I live a good hour
away and got here in 25 minutes
and all because I thought me uncle
was dead or sumthng. '
She looked all surprised
and said, 'Ahhhhhh not much,
sweetheart. There's been a few real
bad fires over the back there in the
pine plantation!'
'Your joking!' I shout back.
'So what's that gotta do with

bad reception from people not calling ya back???'

'Yehhhh,' I said. 'Quite annoying, really as I was worried sick about me old uncle who only just lives up the road.' But she just looked and smiled at me and asked if I was paying with cash or card!!!!

'Well it depends up here I heard you serve free nuts with purrrrr purchase,' I said with a faint stutter, 'and I got outta here.'

'Was yehhh, they're $2.50 with every drunk asshole I meet.'

I laughed and said, 'Nahhh

don't do that I must have just
read the sign wrong back there.
I think it was a big bags of chips
you hand out so I'll just give you
the tip for now okay darls, see if
you can handle that...' I muttered
under my breathe!!!!! She took my
change, grabbed the slab of beer
and took off quicker than "White
Lightning Couriers" up the road
back to uncles. I parked the car up
top of his steep, freshly concreted
driveway and proceeded down
with one bag of chips, slab in hand
and a pocket full of nuts. Little did
I realise what was even more nuts
was about to soon follow.

I knock at the door, he opens
up and says, 'come on mate, in
ya get. It's been a hell of a week
and not over yet. It's good to see
ya, now crack me open that beer,
boy and let's chat the night away
but not so much my troubles.
So pull up a chair and listen to
this... ohh and before I begin,' he
says. 'Thanks for looking after the
business for the last week or so!'

'No worries,' I say. 'What's
family for, now what's been going
on as I thought you might have
died or something?' We cracked
a couple of coldies and he began

our conversation by telling me the reasons why he wasn't at work all week.

'Because I've been busy up home here dealing with a threat from a fire bug!'

I said, 'You're kidding! It's fire season and you're in a very bushy area there pretty bloody brazen to do that this time of year aren't they?'

He takes a sip of his drink and says, 'Yehhhh you're not wrong. Let me tell ya what's been going on.'

'Yeh lay it on. As I said, even the woman down the bottle-oooo who sold me the grog said there had been fires over the back of them further into the pine Forrest.'

'Yehh the mungrels. Not only that let me tell you more...' as we sat drinking our beer! He carried on saying, 'I had not long bought a second hand ute that I had needed for fire wood deliveries for up home here ready to be stocked out in the back block ready for next winter. Anyway, the ute had been for sale from a business that was updating their vehicles, so I got word from my new neighbour that they were selling theirs. You buuuuuute, twin identical utes on the reasonabley cheap side of prices.'

He had got wind of all this from one of the blokes who lived next door. They both had identical paint work and body shape, the only difference was one was an automatic and the other was manually driven. The both paintworks were all white and had thick red shaped stripes down both side quarter panels. The thick red stripes joined up in and over the top of the bonnet of the utes in the brightest of red colours. The story goes that someone one night had walked down the driveway and opened up the driver's side door and with old wrapped up newspapers tried to light them up on the driver's side floor of my new second hand ute! I was surprised to hear if such a thing happening to my uncle, having a fire bug attempting to burn things up in and around his home late at night.

'So that's why,' my uncle said, 'I had been staying up really late most nights to try and catch this person or persons in the act!'

'Well, I'm now staying over for the weekend and will help you

take shifts in catching the fire bug.
You need to get some sleep.' We
had cracked a couple of beers and
sat to eat dinner. There sat me, my
uncle and his de facto wife – we
were the only people in the house.

All three of us had sat after
dinner and I said to my aunt, 'You
can have a decent night's sleep
tonight as me and uncle are taking
turns in shifts throughout the night.'
We decided to take a walk around
his home to chat more about who
it could be? The burning question
was how it could be anyone! We
had also thought that maybe the

fire bug had mistakenly targeted the wrong ute to set alight as the next-door neighbours was too identical, in case there was a mistake in identity from the would be "fire bug".

There was now another car at the top of the home driveway. My uncle's home was dug down deep with a steep driveway on a sloping block and so his home needed a retaining wall, full-up to six foot high sleepers around the front of the home and running along like an L shape down the other side of his home, opposite the

driveway. It, too, was six feet high
in height full-up of surrounding
retainer wall sleepers, all because
of the steepness of the block and
to stop any landslide of earth falling
back into the newly built home.

His home had water tanks
and those used town water. Down
the side of the house there were
two extra-large bottles of natural
gas for the home and in the back
it had its own jacuzzi with decking
under the veranda and a huge,
twin 4-car garage on the other
corner of the home. My uncle
had also owned the vacant block

directly at the back of this block, so we walked over and took a look around at length for any possible overgrown dry grass.

Well, it had finally reached late into that night when my uncle had heard a noise followed by a scream coming from the house. Quickly my uncle and I took off running back to the house to find that alongside the side retainer walls there had been some holes naturally sawn out of them from being first produced from logs. We then heard from his wife that she had heard a noise from

down that side of the home. Upon
further inspection of the home
and surroundings we found that
there was, firstly, no-one in sight
and the double-storey homes built
either side of my uncle's house,
had no sign of anyone over their
fencing lurking or listening in to our
conversations.

His neighbours who did have
a bird's eye view from their homes
looking down into my uncle's place
had also come outside and said
they had seen nothing and saw no
one hanging around. But what they
had noticed was rather strange, as

we came across bird's seed that had looked to be shoved into the sleepers of the retainer wall holes. They had tried lighting them up with a possible lighter type device or possibly a blow torch. You can even get handheld ones over the counter these days at any servo!

So after chatting with their next door neighbour who seemed a nice fella, who had sworn he had seen nothing, so during our conversation we realised that these sleepers would not catch alight as they were a slow burning material made of treated pine that with their thickness, which was 250ml that they would simply smoulder and not burn like a camp fire set up as such. Also, during this conversation one with the neighbours, I mentioned, 'It must be kids that are doing this, as they don't seem to know that much of lighting a fire.'

In case it was the neighbour of course, we waited for a reaction from him as it was a rather great idea to check for reactions from almost an interviewing line of questioning, as things quite literally were heating up around the uncle's home. I did in fact find that this neighbour had no reaction of panic or guilt or sympathy from which it may have actually been him that was the possible "fire bug". But it was to our amazement that he was some kind of a biological chemist, he quite openly told us but yet we could not rule him or anyone else out from being this fire bug! Also, quite obviously due to his knowledge of certain mixtures from all lethal combining chemicals and so on.

Anyway, we go back to patrolling and nothing else happens that night, the whole next day we get rest, besides me and uncle decided that surely tonight no one would be back. But just in case I said, 'Once it does get late in the night I will stay outside on my own, while both you and my aunt rest as I slept during the day'. So all three of us had a plan that whilst I was out on patrol now with the neighbour on the other side of their house, I must have got wind from other neighbours or uncle of a possible fire bug during neighbourly conversations. The deal was that I would be hiding out in the bushes out the front of the driveway unseen to all. The other neighbour who also had a full bird's eye view from his front porches, could see down the whole front of the house and also downside of front door side of uncle's home. So the deal made with uncle's wife who couldn't sleep that night to find my mobile and stay inside as I would come running down the driveway and see what was possibly there. Down I went hiding in the bushes for a few hours now, as there was nothing in sight or not even a rustling of birds. It was a totally silent night.

Until I heard the next-door
neighbour's door open that I
hadn't yet spoken to about these
surrounding fires, so I wait a
few more minutes as I keep a
keen watch on any movement
to come from his porch as it too
from the front was covered to
the main street by all vines and
creeper type plantation. So I kept
a look out waiting to pounce on
any such movement or sound, I
wait back lying belly down in the
bushes. Pitch black, I continue to
look through binoculars I also had
found in my car from horse racing

event, but in the dark of night I soon found out that distance night vision without lighting was next to nothing.

Time passes, it's been at least 10 minutes now and neighbours have still not made a sound to re-enter the home, I think nothing of it as I'm sure he's a smoker. Now it starts to drizzle, it was getting late and as I walked out from behind the bushes. I now come to walking over the top of the driveway when I saw the neighbour finishing his smoke. He kindly says, 'hey mate you want a coffee or tea?'

I think to myself that I should
not go in for a tea or coffee in case
the feeling I got was something
happening and I will not be able
to see, but as the drizzle began
coming down it got thicker
and I thought why not go in for
a quick cuppa and if anyone
hears something from inside
uncle's home they will ring and
I'll come running. So I go in and
the neighbour puts on the kettle,
we began to chat and he puts a
tea bag in my cup and before you
know it – it's weird actually – he
said he would now go outside and
keep watch whilst leaving me in his

home alone to finish making my own tea. I'm aware now if anyone calls within this timeframe I'll know it could be him or someone he knows that could be trying to set something up?

Sure enough, the kettle hadn't even finished boiling and I got a phone call from uncle's wife. I pick up she said, 'I've heard a noise down the side of the home.' I run straight down from neighbour's house and noticed he is not on the porch, so I go running down the side of house but there is no one there.

I soon hear my aunt open up the side door with uncle now awake and then I said, 'call him out here,' as I run around the other side. I meet the neighbour holding a broom stick, but in his shock of meeting me run around the corner, he half-heartedly tried to defend himself. I soon snatch it from him and call out to him to move out the way and asked what were they doing here?

He replied, 'I too had heard a noise and went to take a look.'

'Well thanks for nearly brooming me to death but I dare say it's time to head back up to your own home again as the coast seems clear down here.' We then on decide nothing major going on as we all head back inside each other's homes as we too had decided there again wouldn't be any further chance of fires tonight due to further fine drizzle beginning to fall. In the meantime I remember only me and my uncle had truly trusted one another had said nothing to nobody about us calling into Dick Smith and buying motion and heat detectors for around the side of the house, where there were the two huge natural gas bottles that used to get changed

over from gas suppliers every
month. We thought to set them
up there as if in the same side of
the house where the sleepers and
retainer walls had tried to be set
alight. So with me out on the couch
and aunty in their own bed.

I was first awoken by the dog
barking really loud and vicious like,
then soon after I heard woooooo,
wooooooo, woooooooo, our motion
detector hidden just outside had
gone off. Bang, up I jump. I yell
whilst still in the house, 'Uncle, get
up the detectors gone off!' Bang,
in a hurry I smashed down the fly

screen door, jump straight through it and see no one out the back. I then in turn put my attention to a smell looming from down the side of the house, woooosssshhhhhh it's there I see a milk crate container, sitting on top of the two gas bottles. Sitting on top of that was a huge no name "savings" branded tuna tin and on top of that was an already lit, slowly burning cigarette. It was only seconds away from burning down over the tin and falling into the tin, and it both smelt and looked like inside the tin was a highly flammable liquid mixture that was sitting three quarters full inside.

It was nearly quite ready to ignite, if I hadn't of made it around the sideway as quickly as I did surely the circumstances would have been much different to saving the day so to speak. It was a daring attempt to have lit a fire spread across the two huge natural gas bottles which would have gas also running through all pipes which were all running down into inside not only the home's walls but also all of the gas appliances. They all would have went off with a huge bang from explosion and all went up in flames and exploded, including all attached internal wall piping and quite possibly burning down the entire home. In speaking of such devastating circumstances I can't not mention that it was also highly likely that all lives within the home and possible surroundings could have been lost from the impact from this more than likely sparked explosion.

So in any case, I took the lit, slowly burning cigarette from off of over the tuna tin mix of chemicals as the only thing left holding the cigarette over the tin was now only already burnt soot or ash left from burning cigarette. Now, as I

removed the cigarette and step on
it to put it out on the concrete floor,
I then placed the tin down over the
back of retainer wall sleepers so
I could continue with now family
questions and shock inquiries as
they headed outside to inspect all
the noise and commotion. They
too were all shocked to see such
a setup attempted on what could
have and surely would have cost
our lives. They, too, could now
see the cigarette and tuna tin,
and what I had done to put it out
and narrowly save our lives! We
were quite lucky we had thought
beforehand (my uncle and I) and

told no one of setting up those motion detectors in the backyard over sleeper walls in garden facing downside of the house where the gas bottles were kept! We were lucky we had set them up only earlier that same day! Otherwise, we might not be standing here all together right now!

I dare say I was also very lucky as where I was resting inside the home at time of possible explosion, I was only 3 metres away, sleeping inside on the lounge couch, from where explosion would have penetrated the entire

side wall! Boooooommmm I
had thought, plus all piping and
appliances such as the stove,
wall oven etc were nearby. So
life fortunately goes on even for
me, the author of this book. I still
to this day I am very lucky to still
be around to perhaps even write
such true crime stories, but in any
case, life does go on and as my
story continues as it was quite a
shame that the screen door I had
kicked in to quickly get outside
did not make it and unfortunately
was put and laid to a scrapheap in
heaven!

Also in continuation of this story a special thanks to these and all people surrounding such personalities or businesses. Firstly, thanks to my uncle for suggesting such motion detection. Also, a special thanks to an old "Bitch" of a dog for her loud bark, she was now sure to be a lifesaving, "Rhodesian Ridgeback". A special thanks to all inventor type people for the wonderful invention of "Motion Detection" and so on and fourth! Thanks again too for reshaping to keep people of this world "Alive"!

So in continuation of this true crime story, the police and

fire department were both called
out as they were ordered to clear
all the scene from any hazardous
materials and collect any evidence
they may have discovered. But
realistically they only ever took
off with a tuna with accelerant
and a cigarette bagged up along
with milk crate as evidence. So
as you can imagine there was no
more sleep for quite a while as
no one had been caught so all
we did was simply stay around
home and merely wait for further
things to unfold.

All our phones had been charged in case of further crimes being committed. I remember waiting up outside the uncle's home and there was also a now freaky feeling of having the same drizzle of rain come down from a few nights previous and with me now having no sleep from all last night. I was soon to be like all in the home – deliriously tired – and kept thinking surely with the rain no one would ever consider lighting another fire. This time uncle too could see I was tired, he was resting on the couch this time and I had come in and said, 'Uncle, I'm

tired. I'm going to sleep for a few
hours, in the bedroom next to your
main bedroom.' He said goodnight
to me and I said, 'if you hear
anything yell out, I'll come running.'

'No worries,' he replied with
a concerned look upon his face.
I then walked past the bedroom
where their door was slightly ajar.
I noticed his wife still awake sitting
on the bed, having what looked
to be beer with what looked to
be a medicine bottle with a cap
removed sitting up alongside the
bedside table. I was concerned
about seeing this but I too was

young and thought not to say anything as I knew we were all stressed out! So I continue on to next bedroom to get some sleep while uncle Peter was to be up keeping watch. I fall asleep!

'Bang!' I don't know how long I've been in deep sleep for, but I had just been woken up to what I could only be describe as the loudest death scream I had ever heard, it sounded like my aunty Joy Bering was being attacked! Her scream so loud to have woken me from a deep sleep, to the point where almost felt like she was right there in my

room yelling in my ear. I could feel
the fear from my room and I had to
find my aunt to help her as I had no
idea what she was screaming for. I
had heard my aunt Joy's frightening
screams and I raced out of my
room and quickly headed down
to where I could hear her scream
getting louder. As I passed her main
bedroom at a glance, the door
now open and no one was inside.
I continued running down the
hallway from the main bedrooms
and I look down the hallway. I saw
uncle Peter had been and was still
out on the couch. He had his back
to me, so I yelled 'Pete, get up!'

He started to wake up as I could start to see him move from the couch, as I continued down the hallway. I came to see a huge flash of light come from outside the washroom laundry screens door, and found it was there I could see my own aunty Joy on fire screaming for help. She was standing just outside the laundry door outside the screen door – she was burning. As quickly as I could I opened the door to her and found that her head, face and whole lower and top mid-drift of her body was totally on fire! She was screaming so loud it was a

frightened to death scream, almost
deafening. To see and to hear her in
the way was quite the shock! As I
began to think quickly in the shock
of seeing what was happening
before me I acted quick upon not
even being able to think no more.
I put my bare hands straight into
a patting like motion all over her
head, neck, chest and stomach
regions of her body where she was
literally melting from the burns of
raging fires upon her whole entire
upper body.

I had now put my hands all
over the once-burning areas of

her body and she was now flame-free! Her melted skin and clothes had dropped like a waxed candle and had both melted together at a site. She was in trouble and as I devastatingly looked on at least now I had to put her out! She was not looking good and as I just finished putting her out she had literally fallen into my arms! It was from there I could see and feel she was in shock from all that had just happened to her. She was now in my arms from a possible faint and collapse, she historically begins to talk to me as I now begin to carry her in from outside, as I am carrying her inside I tell my uncle to call for all emergency services.

Now everyone's distraught as I came to carry her over to lay her down onto the couch, I could really see once more up close that her clothes once again had melted into her burnt skin and you could really see her skin had lots of damage from the fire's flames. They had caused a downward melt down from all affected areas: her head, face, neck, chest and stomach regions! As she was now really badly burnt! Still in shock from what has happened to her, she was now laying on the couch trying to talk about what had happened, in shock she firstly said 'he's a big man, grey hair, blue jumper and has glasses! Still in shock she now changed her story as if now to say, 'ohhhhh no, I've done it haven't I? I've fallen asleep with a lit cigarette on the bed again haven't I?' Aunty Joy was coming and going, in and out of shock! As she would continue both stories as she would also continue to say sorry, sorry, sorry. Buy as we all waited for the emergency services to arrive all we could try to do was comfort her.

I remember listening to her stories of how this could have happened to her. I had already ruled out her falling asleep inside on the bed as she was found to be outside! So I knew this was just her in shock! But as for the man she described, I had now noticed that while we were waiting for emergency services, he had come down to see if anything was alright. Finally, ambulance officers arrived to help treat her, so I carried on outside chatting with the neighbour that had come down as he was now talking with police. He states quite clearly and concisely that he had seen Joy from below where he was standing up on his double story veranda home from where he had a bird's eye view whilst outside. He, in fact, had seen Joy throw something over herself and light her own self up! That would now make sense as to why she described him and all he was wearing and a brief description through her shock of burning herself! As for Joy, she got carried out onto a stretcher bed by the ambulance officers who had said they were now off to take her for further treatment to the Northern hospital back in Epping which was Melbourne Victoria's closet 24 hour emergency hospital.

As for me and uncle Pete we both stayed behind at the house for the further crimes unit to finish clearing all crime scene of fingerprints, medications, alcohol bottles and yet another tuna tin and box of matches left thrown away outside the sideway to the now captured yet infamous and self-torched fire bug criminal – Joy Wilson! As forensics did come back and of course all evidence led to Joy Wilson in fact being the Waterford Park/Clonbinane "Fire Bug" as forensics did state within their own finding that she had poured all content of tin over herself in an upward angle which determined it was herself that then struck the match to therefore light her own self on fire! Once all emergency services had left me and uncle still feeling pretty distraught after what had taken place, the two of us then decide to head to Melbourne and visit to see she was ok.

The worst thing I can remember after that was I must

have been reaped by someone,
as I also do remember forgetting
it was even Joy who was the fire
bug. I remember down the road of
life being somewhat branded by
the whole event and even being
somewhat forgetful as to even
think it may have been my uncle's
fault. That he, in fact, may have
caused this firebug situation, but it
just shows in the shock and terror
of things that even, yes you the
reader, and me the author shouldn't
always believe what's around you
only, what's in front of you in an
actual factual state of mind! My
ex-aunty had her problems and

as we all do, did not harm anyone but herself in the end. As my aunt and uncle departed and split from their lives, all I know now is even in dealing with such pain we can still further on in life lead someone's thoughts astray. In saying such things, I did still save not only my life but surely other people's lives and I will try not to be brain dead to other people's circumstances, as I do love my family and I do respect my uncle "Peter Da Painter" and what a life we did share!

TIME FOR AN
IN-TIMER

I have been thinking of my
own life and how quickly
things can get away from you;
like for instance, when I had
been forced to learn something
somewhere which I had never
wanted to learn in the first place,
which I was never going use
myself, in a way others would
have liked purely for their own
benefit and now I have turned
all that around and have ordered
gifts. To those that have heard me
and would like to gain something
for themselves, other than those
taking away from decent people

who have been struggling to learn something of either a "Satin" or "Allah" following.

I am not either and I find all or both follow ahead of times, while they feed off of others. I find that using none of their ways is useful to me as I do not feel I'm a follower. Anymore of any such of their beliefs as they have none they like me choose to act upon what needs to be done in order to get what is possibly already on the way.

I prefer that my strong belief is not to follow any of anyone's own beliefs, and I feel it is about time

they do learn to respect others and
what they have now set in place
within their own body of life. It is
for a better life and therefore a way
of having to deal with who you
will all find to be either friend or
foe, within mapping out your own
life, without having to ask for too
much along the way as I am too
grateful for what life has had to offer
rather than in the form of one huge
learning centre of this our world.

As they too all gifted to save
face I'm speaking of "Satin" and
or "Allah" but as do I for mapping
out what it is I am to do within my

own life's choices, without feeling the need to follow anything other than what it is I do without having to ask. The gift is simply given to those that find those that have done harm either towards myself and/or planned that for others and so on as fourth is a number in-time, people may stand to lose more than that they feel is there fourth in, due to all that can and will be spoken of. Not only spoken of but replayed to the fullest on a daily basis and as for gifts, they also speak up of the knowledge of someone else's thing. Depending on their own severity in which we all hope to find the exact truth as to why they were forced I'm sure to take or harm others, including the internals of myself will stand to lose all that they have come to gain, depending on the severity of such crimes committed speaking of those that follow ahead of times.

What of you when you continue your ways, how long before you are brought back exactly to what and where you should have been now long before after that. Will you have left with all you love and cherish the most? My answer is it's always just a matter of time and now all have this exact power, due not only to what has been mentioned but also to those that have the power of a replay. Now I start the clock on what has you now keenly listening the most, what are you going to loose from what you have either done, ordered or been ordered to do as such? So in time either now or later on in one's afterlife what is it you will all hear, what is it of a somewhat materialistic nature that you feel is more important to you, that will see all taken away from what you' have done? Ask your own selves what materialism of in which you have gained, that cannot be taken with you? Ask yourself what is it now that is important to you?

Once again speaking of time, what in comparison to one's life is most important as material objects, that cannot come with you, what is it then that you hold dearest to you for all eternity, will now then never be again for all of eternity? Once answered, think of time and not only of time, think how much do you already share with those you will all come to loose, your most loved, most dearest to you after all? I say to you all that have been taken from me I love you all my most precious of all, see you when I'm there! You will have all the time in the world with those you love the most, it is all just a matter of time. Lucky for me I have no children and or no materialistic ideal of which I cannot take with me anyway! So I too think of time!

So for those that will be spending all eternity and be thinking of time, I say about time you understand and now you learn why it is those that do good pass on, all I will say for myself is about time as I've had all mine taken

and I'm knowing now I've got this
feeling of being left behind, being
left without and all for the materials
and ideals for what may seem a
better life. I am too far behind in my
own life here and now because of
all that has been going on for far
too long, but when thinking of time,
I will in time still somehow hope I
already have created something
for many others to know and or to
hold their heads in shame and/or
high. That in time I could choose
to move on from this hell of a life
as I'm now aware I'm not hurting
anyone anywhere over such an
idea of materialism. I am no longer

a materialistic person due to all this ahead of time business, and I have and still are to this same day have suffered tremendous losses that can now no longer be said to have gained back within my own living life here upon earth.

I had chosen not to succumb to this ahead of time materialism, I am choosing to still live out my life as nothing more. Still to this day I cannot and will not ever achieve anything much more than this hell of a life I have been made to live. I will no longer – nor will I ever – succumb

to such devastating ideals for
a better life as I have had a slot
taken from mine, and I only now
think of time as "about time" and
realise all I am is all I can now
do. Even when the possibilities
of further takings from my life
exist, I will have at least at very
best wrote and understood this
for not only myself but for those
that have had the same things
taken throughout their living life
here on earth. All I have left now
is time and even when (or if) I die
tomorrow I choose as I fought
hard to live a non-threatening,
non-materialistic life.

I'm not that happy, I'm not that sad, I'm just simply thinking of time and how precious it is in any way, shape or form as all I have or can afford is putting my pen to paper and I can afford to live the rest of my life now it cannot be returned, in a non-idealistic yet nonmaterialistic way. But in my defence and in the defence of others that this unfortunate series of events had led to, we still all have shared time in this life to try make our lives count, even when you have nothing, we simply do not want anything apart from that which we all deserve anyway. For the afterlife I know I will come to pass, as I have got the strength to make it through a hell of a living life to get there, wherever 'there' is when I'm gone from this life. I know now and when I'm there I will have been one of those who has earned their rightful spot with whom or with whatever I've got.

I hope you all are and have listened carefully to my story. When thinking of time, what is it that you find is most precious of all? So really think of what to do now and in-time, from an in-timer. I'm not ahead of anyone and/or anything and I Justin Daniel Broughton am happier I've turned out like I once thought "richer in many ways", but not for an idealistic and materialistic way of life as the only precious things I can take are what we all are together in "the afterlife". I mean no disrespect to all. As I truly am simply an "In-Timer"! See you all when we get there, in-time and not a moment sooner! The end is in-time and the beginning is on time for the afterlife.

IN-DIFFERENT
TIMES OF PLANNED
CHAOS, THE DATES
REMAINED
THE SAME!

Well, I was 18 years of age when me and a friend decided we would go sign up to complete a security course together. In doing so we both ended up "smack-bang" in the heart ♡ of Melbourne's CBD. We had all the excitement of young men about to embark upon life's gift of a journey spent together; shared as two friends from high school starting out their working careers. We had entered this course for good reasons, one of which was for work and the other for having the ability to choose a different career than one chosen by our parents.

As it was, my friend was not so keen to take the opportunity of helping with the new family business of running a tip truck with a skid-steer on the back (similar to a bobcat). This machine was to be sent out for jobs that involved cleaning up of and expertise of levelling house blocks. But that wasn't what my friend wanted to do, so I guess, like me he chose to do security. I thought it would be a great opportunity to have a change

from not making any money and
for helping others change their
disruptive ways of behaviour whilst
out and enjoying the party scene.
So I guess I had made a change for
the better in the life of myself and
a friend that would ultimately be
helping others change their social
decline in the form of drunken
and/or life threatening state of
wellbeing. I remember thinking
to myself there would be more to
write home about from this day
onwards.

We enter the course with
a full class size. We all had to

carry out practical and written work and perform in a role-play situation. We also had to have a sound written knowledge of all laws and procedures. Once all was completed we were all to be assessed. We in the class then moved on to the training side of things, which was being thought to us by highly experienced guards, such as army instructors that made it to retirement. They enjoyed training us younger men in readiness for all our possible security/guard roles to help lead us into the future of an accomplished security guard/crowd controller!

I could see and feel from all the instructors that they too loved their job and they were knowledgeable in the art of security of all types of life-like scenarios.

So we began by having our first real practical sessions, learning such physical manoeuvres like the cobra-lock! It was simply an arm-bar which was a form of wrapping one's enemy or disruptive person into submission to surrender one's bad behaviour. This move was quite effective, and we all soon learned the correct technique of simply striking your opponent into submission to disable one's action of being able to forcefully strike back! Therefore, leaving your opponent no choice but to succumb to our heavy-handed tactics, and the power has simply transferred back to where it should be as now your disruptive opponent has to now succumb to my every lawful order. A job well done.

My instructor could see I had a gift, and now I too could feel the strength and power in who I was becoming. I learned the true value of keeping order among patrons either at a public event (which is said to be a crowd controlling) or securing of premises (when we are forced to be a security guard). Though during the role of security guard patrons and or people of all shapes, ethnicities and genders still need to feel law and order!

My instructor soon saw my sense of empowerment, especially when he along-side his trained colleague both held me in their arm-bar and ordered me as a civilian wrapped up in a double cobra-lock to try and free myself from their manoeuvre.

I felt this was my time to strike and felt my true strength (if you will), to test all I had learnt in a role-playing scenario which has me as cast as the villain. I in front of my entire course cohort, in one swift movement broke free from my instructors which would surely have held a non-trained opponent. Ha ha ha, I broke free of the excitement of the contest to see my instructors. They simply turned to the class and said:

'Well, there you have it. Lesson learned. Some people are just too strong to hold down! Let that be a lesson to you all and now, Justin…' I heard my name called, 'please sit down. Not all scenarios play out the way you would like so it pays to have a sound knowledge of all types of possible scenarios.'

Once the whole class had taken a turn being wrapped up into all kinds of body bars and holds, we were all passed off and assessed. We were all taught correctly without overstepping the techniques we had learned from professional security personnel. We all moved forward onto the final assault of our month-long 8 hour training days to complete our last module before becoming fully trained security guards/ crowd controllers. We all needed to complete our medical procedures unit, which involved being prepared for the treatment of patrons in a life-threatening situation. We were asked, for example, how to treat a patron who has been in an incident and has either been glassed to the face at a nightclub or punched down the pub.

Therefore, we all learned the highest level of first aid procedures, and to pass our finals we were required to have a satisfactory training of resuscitation which is formally known (in the medical world) as C.P.R. Now everyone had been tested, we now had all the knowledge to carry out all medical responses needed to protect our fellow man, woman and child if ever there was a need. So it was assessed by my instructors my friend and I had completed our course and to our delight, we were sent straight down to The World Trade Centre for our governing body so all us new to the security industry could now receive our security/crowd controller licences. So, it stands me and my friend had made it to finally becoming a licenced security guard at the age of 18.

I was lucky enough to have completed this course with a man that had a brother who owned his own security company and, as we were told we did perform quite well during our class, we both would get the opportunity to work for "customs" as guards. We were to check all employees and patrons who entered the building and they all had to wear their security passed to enter and exit this government facility. We enjoyed working there, me and my friend, as there were now two young but enthusiastic 18 year old security guards at the helm of such an important Government institute. We both kept well enthused by our new job as there were plenty of young women that also worked there, so we carried out our duties of making sure all passes were current and visible at all times.

As the weeks rolled on the shifts rolled out and we were doing better than expected. We were hearing some great feedback from the brother of the owner, the guy we had done our course with. We were still learning and earning our way through life which is what we wanted, when one day I received a visit from the security companies director and he was in need of another two guards for the securing of another facility, so we both decide yes we're in! We walk over and he began to show us the ropes. We were to do much of the same tasks, like checking all of the badges and passes of those who wanted to enter this facility, also government property. We also had

to have proof of all security passes,
as there were now internal security
also watching out for those who
were denied access to this building
for security purposes. Therefore,
all internal affairs were sparked by
IA which were ranked quite a bit
higher than us new guards were.
So the nights were much the same,
we would complete our rounds
on a daily basis, and our nightly
routine involved making sure that
all patrons that had gained access
throughout the nights were still
internally accepted.

As certain personnel could still be issued a non-entry compliance due to unforsaken circumstances left unspoken but not unnoticed, as orders from upstairs IA security had just handed down orders downstairs. We did, however, need to be informed through the buildings upgraded technology systems which helped us keep informed due to an overnight lockout system override that would be uploaded and updated every minute of every hour to keep this buildings secrets secure. It was and still is uncertain times and the challenges the people and world face are only growing – times were definitely changing.

Well, anyway, that was only a brief part of my job. My friend even experienced this firsthand and had not been allowed back into the building when he was demoted back over to customs which was over the road. I had been promoted to day security which had a higher volume of securing involved. I didn't mind, as I was sure the days would seem to go much quicker than working on the nights. Work carried on for a few weeks and I remember one day I was sitting inside the security station from where I was working a government building. Now, this was a sunny day and there seemed to be the air of quiet come over the normally heavy trafficked building. It was lunch time I thought and perhaps everyone was busy on lunch. I continued to log documents to other office personal as they were soon going take off. Until I suddenly noticed an old, late-model green car pull up outside the entrance and stop a further 10 metres up the road. A person jumped out of

the now parked vehicle which I
thought looked rather suspicious as
I had never seen them before and
their body language was distinctly
nervous upon entering the building.

In this building I would stand
to secure it from behind 3-inch
thick bulletproof glass, totally
secure from any initial gun fire,
so out the front of the foyer glass
window there was a speaker
button for the intercom for normal/
general public to use as they were
not permitted inside this building
apart from the viewing upon
the front foyer which held the

Australian Federal crimes museum. So I had noticed on the way in this suspicious looking Muslim person was holding an A4 sized, yellow letterhead and as they approached the front counter they began to push the speaker button.

I felt they were panicking; I could tell because of their form of hurried speech. They sounded quite rehearsed as they spoke in a non-English tone and manner. They appeared to rush their sentences as if not to forget what they had to say. He first said, 'I have information on a certain terrorist

plot and inside this envelope
obtains this information. Can you
pass this on to your supervisors?'

He spoke with great haste
and it was still rather hard to
understand this man from the
quick, rushed way of his ethnicity
of speech. It was nearly impossible
to fully understand him. I had
begun to question him and asked
him, 'what is your name? Calm
yourself...' He was quite agitated,
and he did not tell me his name
which intrigued my own suspicious
mind. He then in turn interrupts my
interview by changing his story.

The envelope no longer holds any information for my superiors, it actually contained a form of highly lethal white powder called Anthrax. He continued to talk on, appearing rather high strung and clearly stated this package was highly lethal and could kill when exposed to the open air as the oxygen could enhance its lethal durability.

I therefore said to this person to calm down and tell me exactly who he was. He left the A4 sized letterhead envelope on the front counter and then proceeded to run out the building. He jumped straight

in the getaway vehicle which
was only ten metres away from
building's entry with someone who
was still waiting in the driver seat
with engine still running. They sped
off in a really big hurry. All I could
do was risk my life, risk a possible
"Anthrax" poisoning, so I could do
my duty and get the make and
model of the vehicle and take
down the car's registration from
the quite possibly stolen plates
and/or vehicle. The alternative was
to do nothing and further protect
myself, but I thought it was my
honourable duty to risk such a
toxic poison scare.

I had now come in contact with the possible "Anthrax" envelope as I had made the decision to call their bluff and bring the package inside the quarantined area of the building. I called in a possible threat of terror and was now in lockdown. I then called upon IA to further help investigate they were now on their way down from reviewing all footage and clearing the package (hopefully) from any harm to allow buildings and any passers-by to be clear and free from an Anthrax outbreak. Once cleared my superiors praised

me on a job well done but the
building was to remain on further
lockdown the night and into the
morning.

I did my rounds as per
normal throughout the hours as
day soon turned to night. Night
soon changed to morning and it
was time for my final routine check
of the building and then await the
further shift change of guard. I took
a further 30 minutes to secure the
whole building. As I was doing my
rounds I was thinking I wonder
what episode of Thunderbirds
thcy would be showing on the

idiot box this morning, as it had been a long shift with all possible terror attacks having been taken care of. I always finished my shift by watching the monitors and screens and they had allowed one of them to be used for normal television for us guards to watch.

Anyway, my last routine check had me catch the lift back upstairs to where I was now stationed for a change over in an hour. As I enter the room in which I'm stationed I find the television was loud and I noticed all was well on the monitors. Then I noticed

it looked like there had been a
cancellation of Thunderbirds
and instead it looked to be an
action movie I would soon be
watching. The TV was showing all
different angles of an aeroplane
flying through the air nearing
dangerously close to two tall
buildings that were skyscrapers.
Before I knew it, before I could
even believe it, my eyes witnessed
that plane not even deviate and as
the camera angles changed, the
aeroplane had suddenly smashed
into one of the tall buildings. This
was soon followed by a vision of
a second aeroplane also crash

landing high up into the second skyscraper.

It was from that moment on I knew this was no movie I had ever seen before. I was watching what was and will always and forever be remembered as '9/11', September 11 2000, the twin tower terror plot live on air. It was shocking to watch but even more so after realising there were now reports of a possible Pentagon air strikes from undisclosed terrorists. I now realised I was watching the terror live from America's terror plot where thousands were killed, with reported damages estimated into the billions. From where I was watching in Australia the date had now rolled over into September 12 2000 and I had just worked through our own home-soiled Anthrax terror plot. But it occurred and will also always be September 11 2000 when this occurred.

I was now watching a time in-differentiated terror plot unfold from another country, which is allied with us during war times and in Governed crimes. I had now worked through my own Australian September 11 Anthrax terror plot which was being processed throughout, despite all the possible criminal intent watching online air television hours later. This was on the same date, technically, that information on such a plot and or possible show of fear from Anthrax threat had been discovered in Australia. It was now, in fact, an in time in-different country of America's reality of a terror plot.

Time is important and most precious of all is what can or does happen to an indifferent time on the same date of the World's order, being the same now, then and

always will be, absolute chaos
(even organised chaos if you will)
are indifferent but dates remain
the very same. The end is always
hard to write as I know what has
already been written is sometimes
very hard for any one man like
myself to swallow, but it's true. Now
I feel I am much older and yet I
have seen and/or lived through
some devastating times, if only
to say indifferent times the dates
will always remember for terror
that day, this day September 11. All
dates of terror all remain the very
same. All though my life it seems
had no purpose or much meaning

like most. I feel life is much more than just knowing who one's self is, but also knowing what's around you. You may not always be as it seems in that or its entirety, but yet all somewhat dangerous the same. What is true chaos has been brought to my attention and it is exactly what I've wrote – to the exact we are all very much the same if not indifferent our times (the dates) still remained the same. All that makes us the same now is the intended time difference for chaos, to be what was the same only a time indifference. Chaos all the same.

THE

END